To Dear Quaakie

LINE OF DRIFT

with love &

Robyn Rowland

friendship &
in hopes for more
meetings,

Doire Press

love
Robyn xx

First published in May 2015

Doire Press
Aille, Inverin
Co. Galway
www.doirepress.com

Layout & cover design: Lisa Frank
Cover image: *The Poet's House* by Vera Gaffney
Author photo: Lynda Burke

Printed by Clódóirí CL
Casla, Co. na Gaillimhe

ISBN 978-1-907682-39-1

'Membrane of Air' from *Collected Poems* by Vincent Buckley, published by John Leonard Press. Reproduced by permission of Penelope Buckley.

'Late Fragment' from *All Of Us* by Raymond Carver, published by Harvill Press. Reproduced by permission of The Random House Group Ltd.

We gratefully acknowledge the assistance of The Arts Council / An Chomhairle Ealaíon.

ACKNOWLEDGEMENTS

Acknowledgements are due to the following anthologies and journals in which versions of some of these poems have appeared: *Australian Poetry Journal*; *Westerly*; *Axon: Creative Explorations*; *Quadrant; Canberra Times; Heat; Divan; Arena; Naresh Momdal Magazine Poetry,* India*; Prayers of a Secular World.* eds. Jordie Albiston and Kevin Brophy (Inkerman & Blunt, 2015); *Falling and Flying.* eds. Judith Beveridge and Sue Ogle (Brandl & Schlesinger, 2015); *Australian Love poems, 2013.* ed. Mark Tredinnick (Inkerman & Blunt, 2013); *The Best Australian Poems 2013.* ed. Lisa Gorton (Black Inc., 2013); *The Best Australian Poems 2010.* ed. Robert Adamson (Black Inc., 2010); *Now you shall know (*Newcastle Poetry Prize Anthology, 2013); *Clifden 35: The Clifden Anthology 2012.* ed. Brendan Flynn (Ireland, 2012); *Poetry World: A collection of world poetry* (International Bengali Poetry Festival, Kolkata, India, 2012*); Writing 4All: The Best of 2010.* ed. Fred Johnston (Ireland, 2011); *The Other Voices International Project — US Cyber-Anthology, 2009.* ed. Roger Humes.

'Solitude of Friends' was shortlisted for the Newcastle Poetry Prize, 2013. A number of poems were shortlisted and longlisted for the Fish Poetry Prize 2013. 'As We that are Left' was highly commended in the MPU International Poetry Prize, 2012. A sequence of ten poems was winner of the Writing Spirit Award, Ireland, 2010. Thanks to Kieran Concannon and Mary Lovelle for *Inishbofin: Through Time and Tide,* 1997.

My gratitude to John Walsh and Lisa Frank of Doire Press for their excellent editing of this book, for the lovely design, and for making me cut it! I appreciate their support and interest in my work and am thrilled that Doire is the press to publish my first book in Ireland. My gratitude to the Arts Council of Ireland for a publishing grant, reinforcing my sense of belonging. And to the Australian Copyright Agency Limited for travel grants to read at poetry festivals in India, Serbia and Bosnia.

Thanks to Vera Gaffney for her permission to use *The Poet's House,* a gorgeous painting she completed after my 60th birthday party in Connemara; and to dear friends Ita O'Donovan and Alex Skovron for their reading of my work over the years these poems have collected. Also to Paul Casey for his careful reading of the manuscript and to John Foulcher for his meticulous, sensitive and detailed suggestions on it.

CONTENTS

I Here and There

Island Harvest	11
Solitude of Friends	12
Mayo Mead	16
Lunar Lullaby	17
Burnt Words	18
After Black Saturday	20
Four Poems of Love	
1 Slightly Worn	22
2 Hyacinth Loving	23
3 Invisible Fields	24
4 Shock	25
Golden Flight	26
Garavogue Session	28
The Long Walk	30
Hero Unmasked	32
Thanksgiving for Annagh-ma-kerrig	34
Laying the Ghost	36
Discovering White	39
Autumnal Drift	40
Yarrack Valley of the Wurundjeri People	42
Cuckoo Spring	43
Death Dream	44
Sailing to Cong along the N59	46

II   Unbroken Stone in a Stubborn Sea

Unbroken Stone in a Stubborn Sea – Epic of Inishbofin   49

III   Changing Tides

Mourning   57

Shaping the Dark   58

Night Watch   60

Brief Sport   61

As We that are Left   62

The Space you Inhabit   64

No End to Voyaging – Reading *Nine Bright Shiners*   66

Legacy   68

Puffing Smoke?   70

Changing Weather   71

Outdwellers   72

Winter's Last Crush   74

Three Poems for Susan

    1   Beside the Glass Wall   76

    2   Blue Moon   78

    3   Formlessness   81

Benediction   82

Known by Heart   83

Bright Moment   84

IV   Along the Drift

Afterword   87

Love Poem for Ita   88

The Poem: In Defence of Excess   90

Research Statement for Creative Works to be Submitted   92
for Peer Review

Meditations on Moonlight   94

Driving Back from Knockroe   96

End of the Road   98

The Busy Sky at Five am   99

Once – Again – Still   100

The Light House   102

Singing up Stone   104

Ecstasy – A Seaweed Bath …   106

Departure, Connemara   107

The Line of Drift   108

About the Author   111

Ireland as usual

the soft pads of hands
blessing, or welcoming,

...

no more than a membrane
of air between us.

– Vincent Buckley, 'Membrane of Air'

I   HERE AND THERE

Island Harvest

for Ruairí & Marie-Thérèse de Blacam, Inis Meáin Suites and Restaurant, Aran Islands

Eating periwinkles requires the harvest,
back bent under a slate sky,
seawater, green as jade,
wet sand sloping to the wrack,
Ruairí lifting weed, molasses-dark and heavy
on an island so wild its rock
rises from the ground in jagged slices
striating a sky crazed-blue.

Eating periwinkles requires garlic,
white wine, swift heat,
Ruairí white-aproned,
a toothpick or large safety-pin,
a wrist to slide, twist and connect,
a heart willing to try
winkles, herbivorous, small as a
baby's thumb, that graze on weed.

Eating periwinkles risks addiction
to the shape of conical shells in the palm,
spirals banded in fine threads of chocolate
and celandine-yellow, heated to downy-brown;
to a taste of ocean secrets, and
the sense of having entered an old world
where edible sea-snails are keys to a labyrinth.

Eating periwinkles on Inis Meáin risks
not wanting to turn for home.

Solitude of Friends

for Úna, on visiting Inis Meáin

Here is the place of solitude –
its beginning and its end –
among the rock and the sea casting itself about,
among the stars shifted away by rain
and small night sounds that only come
from other creatures, not human.
Here, you found a place to be common with it,
to find the bowl of self, that
wash as it will with tides and storms,
remains as sure as the walls of *Dún Chonchúir*.

Each day we walk a different path here,
your birthday gift to me.
We carry our soup and griddle bread,
our singleness, our friendship.
Plants are braving a cold spring,
hawthorn and juniper wind-sculpted.
Yet soil that was made by hand over centuries
from seaweed, crushed limestone and sand,
made itself rich by waiting. It flowers now
in colours that make the rainbow over Connacht pale.

Some would find this place desolate –
giant pavements of compacted layers,
breaking cliffs sharp-falling into boiling water,
boulders thrown up from the deep
that waited on a storm to rain them down,
craggy hills with fretted walls,
stone lacework to let the wind through,
a matrix of crocheted borders
that keeps only beasts out.
But we thrive on its purity.

Lichen and mosses that coat
the weary, slate-grey platforms flourish
in the cleanest Atlantic air, all dust and muck
purged on its way, beaten out of it by storms.
There are springs that drop from cliffs to pools
green with light, lisping those concentric circles
that show movement comes out of small things.
Time lives here, and has no fuss with us,
allows just standing to look into crevices,
where the eyes of bluebells gaze out.

Cathaoir Synge, that stone chair where Synge
wrote out an awe of the place, the people,
is older than before his time,
a collection of rocks placed for a lookout post,
raised by men with barely imagined strength.
We sit inside its solid borders on a damp day,
wind biting and impatient with the light.
Being used to living alone in our quiet houses,
we share easily both silence and talk,
you in your scarlet hat and coat, mine bright-blue.

Synge wrote of a primitive people here,
and the romantic notion that hard times were good,
prosperity a sully on purity.
Some of it, of course, was right.
Written with the true rhythm of the place.
But reality was the courage to get into a
tar and timber *curragh* and go fishing for your life.
Or bring turf in from Galway on a wild sea,
or the doctor and priest, knowing one
was likely needed with the other.

Women no longer wear Synge's red petticoats dyed
from madder roots, nor stir their indigo in pots by the fire.
Keeping that close as a memory is not false record.
He wrote of what was authentic in that life:
endurance and facing fear. Nothing romantic about that.
It comes from necessity.
As when they told us our breasts had cells
that had turned sly, caused chaos;
that to save the body, the flesh must be carved out.
Now we carry more scars than those with us.

We learned that bliss is not found in the body,
but happiness is as powerful as
an ocean swell and just as capricious.
That contentment may inhabit a moment when we
walk together the expanse of curved sandy beach
suddenly soft on this rock island,
leaving behind us the only two sets of prints.
And in knowing that when the arctic gulls
dive at us to protect their nests,
we simply change direction.

At late dusk, wine and the taste of sea
from Ruairí's delicate food
remain on our tongues with the easy words.
Straw Island lighthouse is fierce-bright with its
double-pulse, though the Sound is still.
Beyond lies the uncertain sea,
and our Bens blue as periwinkles that
grow in crevices outside this long window
framing a panorama we can't,
we don't need, to take back.

You said once that loneliness is the price we pay
for a certain kind of freedom. This kind?
To move into the world unbound?
To know the nature of islands and move among them;
to arrive and know the fit of this place
as if matched by heart,
stone by stone, silence on silence?
We sit to watch light leave the silver slabs before us,
night drifting in as if a mist,
settled in the quiet companionship of friends alone.

Mayo Mead

Valleys of Mayo are brim-full with sorrel fall.
A shaggy sun has shaken out its coat of wet gold,
showering droplets over the hills near Westport.
Brackloon Wood swells with scarlet spires of Rowan,
and the pliant Rusty Willow, that never weeps, showers amber
among the fiery orange crowns of Downy Birch.
Lord again in a forest renewed, the Sessile Oak,
standing sinewy and tangled with fern,
splays its frayed blood-cherry cloak across the frost-wary skies.
Roads from Letterfrack to Leenane are girdled with
marmalade and treacle braids spilling into the culverts
where chains and torcs of burnished leaf are hoarded.
Winter is coming. The Sheefreys, Bens and Mamturks
bare their bones as retreating mountain grass
unveils shining eyes and furtive brown flanks.
Green has rusted away to float along bold rivers
gathering their strength after a week of still warmth
shouldering stone along as if it were a child's marbles.
Autumn is a warrior ready for the bitter charge of winter hail.
Yet still, this gathering of toffee colours is so strong
its misty breath tastes like mead.

Lunar Lullaby

Shellharbour, NSW

Breast-white, a blue-veined
moon is bulging over-full
against its girdle of black,
the sea's crush of waves
blowsy in its lush cadence.
Beneath, a deeper thrum,
an engine imagined that
drives the whirling globe round.

At midnight, white water
is high and busy on the beach
and way out half-way to the horizon
it still churns, shattered light
all across the sea now,
waves and flat acres alike
silvered as if blue forgotten,
green a memory,
and only the gilt skin moving
toward this house,
all slick and salt wet.

I turn to sleep in the crease of
sarong on a hot night
suddenly soothing cool,
and the silvered sound
of waves-made-moonlight
calms the heated heart.

Burnt Words

'Black Saturday' was named for a series of 400 bushfires in Victoria around 7 February, 2009. 173 people died, 414 were injured, 2,100 homes destroyed, 7,562 people were displaced.

Wind was never useful in a poem,
but flame, now, yes flame was the core –
heart aflame, passion aflame, longing aflame;
love's burning desire, night's candle of soft light, moon's flare,
the altar of Quan Yin with its flickering quiet, flowering stones,
pink shells lit by the glow of tapers.

We knew the world was altering.
We were told – look to the waters, the shoreline,
ice-storms, poles with their melting caps.
No-one mentioned firestorm, air-ignition.
No-one talked of trees raging with their bursting
heads of fire, sky a turmoil of blood-orange air.
That our forest would ignite
fuelled by its own eucalypt oil,
Mountain Ash dried keen enough for self-immolation.

We knew the fire-bombings of Dresden,
human forests burning in Nagasaki.
Yet still we weren't prepared for the earth itself
to turn tenderless, heave up through its green growth
the unyielding heat of 1500 Hiroshima bombs.
Ember attacks hammered nails through metal and skin,
jet-engines roared in walls of fire to deafen the old,
flames sucked oxygen from the air, lungs left slack.

And poems? All that 'burning in the line',
those 'flame on the tongue' images, seem crude.
Too much ash has fallen;
too many boneless burials.
And poems can't undo the burning.
That new language of terror,
all the frenzy of flame, has
burned away my tongue.

After Black Saturday

Torquay Victoria

This morning sea is gentle, sun kind.
Skin takes both upon itself with gladness
and the heart, forgetting in the moment
a dark smoke-haze that seems no longer
to shroud the air, opens in ragged relief.

Walking the shore at Fisherman's Beach,
sand ripples lead toward golden stone circles
tides have uncovered, left when once an eruption
forced open the earth, and coolness captured it.
In the ti-tree scrub lining the beach

small birds are rustling twigs. The roll of wave is
pucked with their small staccato.
Back through Taylor's Park, mixed trees –
wattle, gum and hakea – stand tall and confident,
knowing rain will come.

Magpies warble their carillon into full swing,
the big-band sound of early day. Ravens
rest on dry boughs in their shining onyx coats.
Cockatoos even, seem less raucous, and the gang-gangs
chew their vowels in luscious melody.

Traffic is absent along the park's edge
where one long feather has just fallen, spiked upright,
fluorescent-blue, titanium-blue, a blue-bird's
treasure that, when held flat, gleams turquoise
toward its pale grey shaft, lightly ashed.

So vivid – as if flight were still in it –
as if the bird dipped into deep-blue sky,
and trailing, trawled the heavens to earth.
We can't stop the light pouring into things – or out –
can't stop the earth creating its worst and its best.

Twelve days and still the toll rises.

Four Poems of Love

1 Slightly Worn

So fortunate to know you late in life –
but not too late –
silver fields along your back where nipples can
nestle in comfort lying beside you,
my smallness curved about you,
earth of your skin beneath coffee-brown from
years of taking in Australian sun, its sly sheen,
its murderous intent that had you under the knife twice.
Kayak-muscle into hard bicep,
cycle-calves curved in clumped strength,
your body is a marvel of constant movement.

How fortunate the swell of your belly, that makes
the stretches of mine gleam like silver minnows,
the movement south of aging continents
all the more cherished for their constancy now.
Love is harboured safe in the heart's bruised recovery
where the landscape of past grief,
the pathways of gladness are worn,
and this wornness a welcome comfort
now age brings us to new excitement by surprise.

How amazing to feel so new –
to be apart yet carrying the joy of you,
watching the moon shake herself over a frosted field
while you scorch in unseasonal heat a wide-world away,
waiting for that same moon to bring its light to our bed,
turquoise sea beneath lapping, lapping.
There, where all my journeys end, homecoming full delight,
your arms again the edge of the known world.

2 Hyacinth Loving

Errislannan

and what did you want?
To call myself beloved, to feel myself
beloved on this earth.
                                        — Raymond Carver

God or flesh, Persian poets wooed their 'beloved' as if
there were no greater gift than to be both namer and the named.
Absent, your brown furred body lives in my skin's memory,
laughter recalled is my *uisce beatha*, water of life,
your care, the charge of a sun.
Every morning, alone here but for the thought of you, excitement
tingles in fingertips that tuck in the stray flips of earth
tipped from indigo pots at my door, as hyacinths,
rising from their dark birth-shrouds, go ruffling for light.
Brown onion caps, almost discarded, balance in comedic joy,
a small wonder as they protrude into the ice-blue chill above ground.
Heads loaded with bubbles of scented flower,
they make the sky ache for their pink and blue sweetness.
In the cleft of their companions' leaves thrust toward sunshine,
clear rainwater is caught, meniscus bulging as if curved crystal.
First night back, a pregnant crescent moon slung low,
carried before her the shadow-shape of herself to come.
Connemara's sky was star-crowded and cold –
deep airborne cold – and pure beyond diamond.
Spring is an act of trust – the sky will warm, buds rise and open,
and the great moon sail into her own fullness as a matter of time.
Waiting is the necessity for growth.
All this readies for you, *Beloved*, and when you come
your soft kiss will give me again the first spring-time of opening.

3   Invisible Fields

after Iarla Ó Liónard

One small, one larger below the house,
loughs at evening hold a late blue light
while crumpled earth of stone and tufty bog
gathers dark in. They dare not shiver, these land-laps brim-full,
nor splash their unshed droplets across reeds
still as stick and straight in a breathless dusk.
Slyne Head lighthouse adds the beat from my suspended
heart to its own, its double flash my only compass point
toward the wide coal-black sea between us.

Your voice so close in my ear I cradled it with the phone
as if you had breathed across my cheek in sleep
as you once did, bodies hot with the sweat of love,
springy fur of your brown skin lit by the silk of me. And yet
you struggle to hold me in memory till I return?
How is love then to know whether to stay or go from the beloved
when life must be more than love alone?

Iarla sings his mellow *sean nós* across the dark now,
melancholic ache moves through invisible fields of land and wave.
Coming from old voices beyond a remembered past,
his Irish more deep and sweet and mellow than mead,
he raises from the dead all old loneliness,
to cut in bright as sharp-edged moon piercing the body of night,
scarring a pathway into water fresh and salt, keen as the
sting of missing you, and I too *am weary of lying alone, alone.*
I am weary of living alone.

4 Shock

ghazal in Istanbul

waking, our distant country seems strange my love to me
mountains stand jagged where flower fields would be

rough river and wide with no boatman in sight
beyond, a stretched desert frost-burned of verdancy

familiar old country I know without maps
tattoos of loss score my bones' history

I re-read your words absent honour, bereft of care,
love leaving, sword-edge-sharp, carves a swift vacancy

in darkness, a thief, your words crept in abrupt,
rejoicing in decision you seem thrilled to be free

on crumbled ruins of our future, abandoned, I grieve the
bright world we would sail, compass wrecked at sea

you have another woman before days have time to heal,
shock inks its solitary script, no embellished calligraphy

diminished, *Beloved,* you made yourself *Stranger* to me,
cruel as a lion's claw you rake your heart free

Golden Flight

to Bob Adamson, from the west of Ireland

Still, these days …
I hold tight to what keeps me
alive – a spur-winged
plover in its broken-wing dance,
distracting the hawk from her chicks …
                    — Robert Adamson, 'The Golden Bird'

October in Connemara after Atlantic gales
shred my late petunias, churning sea to growling
as it claws the stones on Ceann Dólainn bay below.
It marks the season's late change, landscape softening,
roadsides rusting away fuchsia and blackberries.
A flock of goldfinches, their wings flickering yellow,
fall like autumn leaves from my power lines
onto newly mown grass, feeding on seeds with gusto,
and I think of you and the indelible 'Goldfinches of Baghdad',
your poem that rode beauty and cruelty into the flames.

Last time we met you took snaps to show Juno the jewels
of a jewfish my father caught and turned into earrings.
We swapped fish photos for months –
Bob and fish, Dad and fish – bigger, bigger.
Since then it's been birds, birds. I watch them feed, strut,
fly through your photos on Facebook.
They stay airborne – rather than being gutted for eating.
I float the world now
as you grow more alive to your river,
so dissolved into its life it inks your veins.

You called me 'Colour Girl' in middle age,
though the girl was long gone.
You had really forgotten me but that didn't matter.
I remembered you in the old days at Sydney poetry tables
all wild and scary with your word-passion.
I didn't know you were just uncaged,
feeling your wings, and we both grew up alone,
but you were older, crazier, braver
and my voice still lost, imagining a life
outside my own loneliness in the country of the Dark.

You read too much, you talked too much,
you lived too hard till your feet finally caught again
in the oyster beds, as the river reminded you
there was solidity in a grandfather past.
I live in a watery place too, both solid and fluid,
my body and soul laid into the land so each mound of me
fits a silent bog-dip, each curve cups a rufty hillock.
Burnished wrack rings Seal Bay with amber
opposite salt-white coral strands and stone
the grey of dolphins, with a hundred times the memory.

Your 'speaking page' is the Hawkesbury River
I travelled over as a kid on the Wisemans Ferry punt,
imagining I was travelling with the three wise men
walking across water. Bodies of moving water have had me since.
You make it a place we can all come to anytime,
feel the 'serpent's breath' even if never spotting it,
learn the miracle of oysters, of oyster-catchers – man and fowl –
the rich unfiltered flow of river life. I envy that belonging.
How torn my own sense of it. Yet here I live inside the natural, 'same as that'.
And birdlife here in the Irish west grows more plentiful each year.

Even the great Golden Eagles of Ireland Yeats never saw –
symbol of wisdom and power for the Druids –
are resurrected, three pair mating in Donegal.
Most birds travel long, long seasonal paths, rejoice in both flight
and landing, then take off again, different in nature and colour
from those wild reds and yellows that blaze my eucalypt alive in Jan Juc.
I can offer you music though – curlews wheeling along ribbons
of song into myth, no more than the creaking wings of
white swans before they glide into my lough
fingering the rushes for danger, their feathers for stray skin.

Skylarks climb vertically, levelling off to barely hover,
singing melodies flute-clear for twenty minutes.
Stonechats call each other in the percussion of two stones struck –
you think you're kicking rocks walking. Kestrels, wrens, robins,
cobalt blue-tits, pheasant heads red among the reeds, massive seabirds,
magpies evenly marked with white splayed wings black-tipped,
that never repeat in their tunes, all harmony, brains working in halves –
one asleep, the other wakeful, alert. Most amazing are cuckoos –
unwooden – chameleons of the nest, male giving out the call
while he waits on her great deception.

Life is full of confusion, but holding onto beauty
in the natural gives our watery presence a firmer grip.
I remember that old table, typewriters, inked fingers,
and am glad that your keen bird's eye
is still fishing for poems that grow fat
along the Hawkesbury banks and deeper in.
Golden Bird of poetry. Irreplaceable.
I think of your hair whitening to the chalk of oyster shells
and I like that. Better to age than to go missing.
It would be a terrible loneliness, if you were not in this world.

Garavogue Session

for James Carty and Francis Gaffney, the morning after 'Sligo Live'
in the Glasshouse by the river Garavogue – with thanks

James leans back languid beside long riverside windows
after a late-night-early-morning session in The Snug
packed too close. Flute hovering barely touches his mouth,
skin only moist with its soft imprint, all sweetness in the breath,
as he plays a slow air drawn across morning like honey
dropping slow, amber and resonant with memory.

Reluctant at first, Francis fingers strings lighter than raindrops
falling carefully on the dipped backs of swans on the river.
Garavouge, *An Gharbhóg*, 'rough youth', it is swift today
twirling with white water on the cascades then whirling
up-river briefly before sweeping across, back along the rocks.
It risks tripping, speed being the careless swing of the young.

The flute is riding now, waves of it surfing, sweeping sure
and slowly easing into the bank where swans should be
sleeping in still water if spinning were not the
motion of this morning. Now breath moves into a jig.
Suddenly the player takes up the day riding the rise into
buoyancy, as back-waves spiral under a sudden surge.

The river rushes. Guitar holds the tune above water.
Then his voice girdles a song, holds the *nn* and *mm*
compressed at the back of the throat in the old way. He sings of
love enduring in hard high places, of the grace of swans
and women, and though it hides inside a mist of myth,
his nightingale flies tireless into the beauty of these unwounded gifts.

The Long Walk
March 1849, Connacht, Ireland

Violet: The Famine? Malone: (with smoldering passion) No, the Starvation.
When a country is full of food and exporting it, there can be no Famine.
  – G.B. Shaw, Man and Superman

The oracle could have foretold it, though the wisdom of Delphi
was always silent in winter and Pythia had long since withheld her voice,
but with Croagh Patrick to the back shoulder without serpents
and the Goddess still hot upon its face with the old ways
you'd wonder all the signs would warn them, walkers grasping for grain, as
                  into the valley of death
                  stumbled the 600

Snow was sheeting across Ben Gorm and the Sheeffry hills,
Mweelrea mountains shuddering under rain,
blight was on the land and the white globes of goodness that grew
in the dark Irish earth had taken in fallen dust from America,
fungus-ridden with stench of starvation through its flesh, as
                  into the valley of death
                  staggered the 600

Children were barefoot in the iced air, their ragged clothes
barely a cover for thin arms, rickety legs, their stomachs round
with hunger, mothers too weary for tears at their cries,
their own voices lost in despair, mouths long unfamiliar with appetite
or taste or something solid; lost long before
                  into the valley of death
                  struggled the 600

In the rage of a storm it was hard to see if skeletons they were, or
walking dead, spirits through which the wind blew as if their bones
were all that held them up, and try though it may,
no wind could play a tune on these bones, only the
clacking beat of a funereal march as
                  into the valley of death
                  scraped the 600

Hunched against the blizzard, Mweelrea indignant watched helpless
as they clung overnight to sheer rock, rough unflowering furze,
waiting for the 7 am attendance ordered by the Guardians, and
let's name them – Colonel Hosgrove and Captain Primrose – who
slept under their down and starched Irish linen as
                    along the valley of death
                    shivered the 600

From Limerick, Cork, Galway food kept leaving for commerce's hungry mouth.
From Kilrush July 1848, 711 tons of Kerry oats, 128 tons of barley.
Ship after ship left fine busy ports laden with bacon, lamb, wheat and eggs,
while Oscar's Wilde's mother hidden in the name 'Speranza'
raged in poetry at the theft of Irish food, yet
                    still in the valley of death
                    waited the 600

Delphi Lodge's table groaned under lunch while the wretched gathered
in front of long dining room windows; and the Guardians ate and talked –
maybe about the terrible weather, the growing cost of living, the poor;
maybe about the comfort or otherwise of their white beds,
while on lawns between them and Dubh Lough
                    in the valley of death
                    huddled the 600

They took but a minute to deem the gathering not poor enough for government grain,
turning their empty hands away. But here the land is full of pity, and the mountains
opened, gathering their bones into its soft peat; wind lifted them carefully in its arms
and blew them easily into Black Lake. Snow cast a blanket over the young,
sea washed others onto beds of Killary sand, and
                    100 only
                    trudged out of the valley of death

Hero Unmasked

for my father, September 2014

We watched old back and white movies on tv
Sunday afternoons in our fifties lounge-room as kids,
ate dark chocolate with sickly green peppermint filling
running over our fingers from blocks that Pop
brought down from Sydney as a special treat.
You loved westerns – 'come *onnnn* the Indians' you'd shout.
It was a ritual. It was family.
We devoured the forties and fifties like sugar.
Man in the Iron Mask appeared in our musketeer craze.
Here was Heroism, Love, Life and Death.

To a man rarely sick, radiotherapy was incomprehensible.
They wrapped your face in cling wrap first
to block eyes and nose tight. Built up layers of
wet Plaster of Paris to shape a mask.
I watched you struggle like all the fish we'd caught, and
remembered clearly the day my brother and I
wriggled you down the boat ladder in Fiji over a reef way out,
your grandkids fluttering along the surface then diving,
two sleek seals, deeper and deeper, snorkel bubbles
erupting through the meniscus of sea.
Turning I saw your frantic dog-paddle, your urgent scratching,
desperate to get back on the boat, lack of breath a broken line to life.
We heaved you back on board where you gulped at air, floundering.
You just couldn't breathe through your mouth.

In the radiation chamber I saw your body arch in panic,
rushed in, talked you through breath after breath.
I told them – 'he won't be able to do it every day for six weeks.'
When the mask was set next day, it was chunky, sightless –
two nose plugs erect, a strange jelly-fish splayed across your face.
Under it a mesh helmet gripped your face, Spiderman's web
clipped into place, locking your head to the bed, immoveable.
They simply said – 'breathe through your mouth.'
Panic sucked the room clear of air.
I gripped your hand, watched that chest squeeze hard.
You said – 'I have to find a way.'

Best part of it all was sitting on your deck at home, watching
the ocean change, birds fill your grevillea and callistemon
with wild colour – rainbow lorikeets, crimson rosellas, honeyeaters –
the simple brown sparrows that fed with you at breakfast,
pelicans overhead in their graceful jumbo flights.
You spent each morning like this – 'bird watching' you called it –
and laughed – 'the birds watch us!' And you found your way.
There, with poetry singing in your head, you started to recite
the old lines of Paterson, Lawson, Kendall, and I'd stumble through,
a small kid's shadow after her daddy's long strides.
Word-for-word perfect you were.

Each session at the hospital you'd recite to make yourself breathe –
lips never silent while the machine whirred,
telling the walls the wonderful poems you grew me up on.
You'd come out and say – 'I got through *Clancy of the Overflow,
The Last of his Tribe* and *The Bush Christening*.'
Or 'I fitted in *Bellbirds* – I think they took longer this time',
and we'd drive to the harbour for coffee and cake
while I churned that you had to face anything mortal like this.
The radiology team said they'd never seen anything like it.
Of course not! They'd never met my father before –
the d'Artagnan, the Robin Hood, the Ivanhoe – of Wentworth Street!

Thanksgiving
– for Annagh-ma-kerrig

Tyrone Guthrie Artists' Centre, Newbliss, County Monaghan

Sweet green crush of cut grass
full-bodied through the open window,
loosestrife, fragrant purple in a soft afternoon,
and honeysuckle, bruising the belly of day,
pull me from my John Jordan Room
towards the lake and island
sailing into a new tremor of breeze.

Emerald lawn with stripes now
where the ride-on-mower's precision
swathed its path through the rich
growth and silent afternoon, tumbles away
from pale terracotta walls and slate grey roof
of a house where laughter and play were part of
Tony Guthrie's stage-magic made real.

Moonfire dahlias glow in the garden,
saffron yellow with their red-flame hearts,
pink lilies loosen their mouths,
and ivy, heavy with story, is holding
the walls close. Space opens here
through room and garden, through mind and body,
for paint, chisel, word, or note.

A shoal of silver light on the lake
stuns the fading day
with its challenge at twilight,
the fern-fine surface shimmering,
wooded-grey boathouse leaning towards last light,
and two wild swans dropping like white rags
leave a bright tear in the lake's smooth skin.

Walk the forest path beneath a sky of green down
where summer still hangs on, where
wind in the ash trees could be a river stumbling or
rain falling; showers on larch leaves might be
grain tumbling through corn; light through birch,
a shadow of that special mist that sometimes
illuminates in its quiet transparency.

This suspended moment,
everything is stilled except the breath
that slips along the tongue, or the charge
that fires the fingers to work
out of the body, as the gift comes, here
where air and water, drumlin and bloom
float into view, hesitate, fluid with time.

Laying the Ghost

for Ethel 'Bunty' Worby, died March 10, 1962, aged 77, Annagh-ma-Kerrig (Tyrone Guthrie Centre)

Unfurled from the fancies of poets and painters
wanting a ghost to lay beside them,
distract them from this difficult work,
they say you wander the house, chill a room,
move objects about because you are lonely, restless
at your brother's refusal to return your body to England.
But to me the quiet of this house is unrippled.

I don't know why I need to set it straight.
But *come here to me now* – Anne, the cook, and Joan,
that child of Edward Daly the Steward you told
not to hang the washing out on a Sunday – they
knew you, used your recipes, took your photo,
brought letters to you every day, none from a brother
who never existed.

'A tiny, tidy Yorkshire nurse,' Joe Hone wrote, and
there you are in old sepia, bottom shelf in the library
with hundreds of family and strangers further back, and the house,
a character itself, changing backdrop to the ever-renewing play.
Small, light bob of wavy hair, a sure smile,
your rings flash in the sun and a heavy necklace
falls down your soft autumn dress.

So tiny beside the six-foot-five Tony Guthrie, his tall sister,
tall wife, and his mother Mrs G – Norah – almost shaking her head
as you all line up in a row, sideways to the camera,
each with hand-on-hip in a vaudeville backwards lean,
with you, slightly distant from the others. A comedy line-up in 1929
just after you came to the house with Norah,
blind from a disease she picked up nursing Belgian refugees in the war.

Next year, there you are coming through the side doorway
stylish in broad-brimmed sunhat, waisted cotton frock,
carrying a sun-umbrella to join Mrs G sitting in the sun
and Peggy, opening her glasses to read. Alone in another,
you look down perplexed at how you came to be holding
two massive wild salmon hanging from the end of criss-crossed rods,
another awkward balancing act you came to know well.

Years later you sit in the drawing room at tea with family,
friends, growing old, maybe after Norah was dead in '56.
But the best photos Joan dug up from her old albums.
All the backstairs mob in small black and white prints –
weddings, hanging out the washing, sweeping –
and you had asked her 'will you take my photo?
With my lilies Joan, to send to a friend?'

In your own garden there you are brush-straight, while
huge-headed flower sprays strut taller than yourself, white
hair piled high, your face another bloom beside their own.
A ray of sun has strobed you through from head to toe,
as if marking you to be dropped among them. Madonna lilies.
Their heavy scent will gather later in vases in the library,
drawing room, wafting through bay windows with the burn of peat.

Norah's companion for thirty years, a choice you made,
to leave the hospital, to work and live that way
in a house full of laughter, fed on astonishment
that creative people could be so robust, so international,
swooning with theatrical passion and fun, yet still returning
to the roots of manual farm life, jam-making, boating on a lake
so blue the ragged swans were never sure if it were sky or water.

That's what didn't fit with the whisper of your body unearthed,
rootless and wandering. That's why I needed Joan and Anne
who'd touched your hand passing the post to tell me –
Colonel Simons the Steward found you, March 10 1962.
Anne remembers the ambulance coming,
that you died in the hospital in Monaghan.

I don't know if your sister Mrs Urquhart came from Yorkshire,
but your godson Dr Jeffrey Steele arranged it all
following your clear hand and clear mind.
Cremated in Belfast, all the staff in attendance,
you were brought back light as air and settled on the mantelpiece
in the morning room. When the Guthries returned from America
Tony scattered you in your garden. Just as you wanted.

Faithful, loved, you left behind *Bunty's Basic Skills no.5*,
a cookbook in your fine round script, drying to paper flakes
in a brown hessian bag; memories of a garden of flowers tall as wheat;
and a moment Anne in her eighties still recalls,
when she asked one amber afternoon, that question
spinsters dread – and you told her – once
you were in love, 'but it never materialised.'

The ghost stories don't seem respectful somehow.
So here it is for you now, loved companion, Bunty, a truth
out of the yellow throats of lilies, and you among the blooms.
It has to be said that you lived and laughed and were happy here,
that you powdered the very soil of the place with petals,
and returned, scattered and light,
curling in the breeze, sun scooping away shadow.

Discovering White

Geelong, Victoria

The settle of winter is upon us
    trees long rusted away.
Passing slowly in traffic,
    once swampy ground
near the river is dry now,
    a pan with thickets
of raw grasses tall suddenly
    in the flat paddock.
You see where the frost has
    quilted the ground,
and the high wild grass
    is a kind of shining.
Not dull white as if the sun is dim,
    weak on it and suffering.
But luminous;
    so dazzling in the early
crisp morning, polished
    so bright it catches a breath.
And flowering there on the frozen heads
    white becoming its own bloom.

Autumnal Drift

i.m Sandy Kirby, 5 August 1948 – 24 March 2011

It's just so tidal.
This March moon larger than ever,
a supermoon, closer,
swollen with gold and pulling, tides pounding,
you ebbing.

Yesterday I stood by our seat on the cliff above the sea,
swell unusually high. Chewing sandstone below,
it was rolling pebbles on its tongue.
I thought of us there, coffees too hot,
swilling it round our mouths laughing,
David spilling with ideas, edgy to get back to work.
Such a retirement!

It's all so tidal really – memory.
You're turning towards me from the washing up
waving rubber gloves to make a point about politics
after David's dinner with its French accent.
The house shuffles into the night of trees,
its mud bricks we all helped to make years back,
nests for insistent kookaburras,
mad kamikazes targeting the window panes.

Even the dam has its own highs and lows.
You'd stand there with late-light lapping it,
rosellas cracking their last seeds for the day
sighing into the dusk with pleasure.

It was tidal really – pleasure.
After the first invasion,
the burn of chemo, the drugs, the rebuilding,
you swam back into life,
painting, learning to play piano,
sluicing your fluted notes into the silence of the bush.
You loved that place at Bellbrae, 'the land',
peace grew into you there among the gathering of friends.
Wary of 'jumping-jacks' – a real danger for you –
nothing much else seemed to make you afraid.

I sometimes ring you there
to hear your voice on the phone's machine.
I went there the day after you flowed away,
wagtail flitting around me, chattering.
Your voice seemed suspended there like mist
no matter what they say – in and out –
breath remains a dewy kiss,
invisible droplets long accepted into the trees,
the lake, the wet memory-marshes,
the summer sky.

It's all just so tidal.

Yarrack Valley of the Wurundjeri People

It was called Birrarung, River of Mist,
when it flowed quartz-clear into the bay
and campfires roasted fish.
My father walked it in the war
when they were making planes
keeping them coming for the boys,
but he couldn't fish then.

Now he tells me his uncle said it's
an upside-down river – 'too thick to drink
too thin to plough.' Must have been upstream
factories, gold-panning, logging, widening.
It's snake-brown and the sky can't get a look-in
across its grubby face.
Still it's a river and
a city's no place without a river,
ships, cargo, passengers trembling
for islands, far-away docks,
a swing around the azure seas.

It's the sky fallen really, scattering
high and far up in the mountains,
dripping through leaves, sluicing across moss,
trailing its way to the mesmeric seductive salt.
Bodies of water, all of us,
coming and going on.

Cuckoo Spring

Errislannan unfolds this early morning
after months of cold spring flayed with hail showers.
Yet here is one sunny day opening in buttery primroses, violets,
sea-pinks mimicking fallen cherry-blossom over
salted rocks melted grey with seals.
My boots crunch a busy rhythm and the wind begins to
give notice of rising. But not yet.

Knee-deep in button-fill bolls of bog cotton,
a languid cow is tearing pea-green grass from the bog,
her munching and ripping, rolls of sound
sluicing along the crisp air. Watching her placidity,
I recall *what peace there may be in silence*
and stand still, waiting for it to complete its gathering
this morning, on this road, between dry-stone walls and shore.

Below, Ceann Dólainn Bay rests from lapping.
The cow raises her head to pause.
Flutters of air, dip into the lough,
drowning in its blue unclouded stillness,
dropped as if earth hesitates in its spinning,
for a moment surprised in self-admiration.

Then, sweeping through the lull across the bog
clearer than ice crystals on the wire fence this month passed,
a cuckoo gurgles wicked delight, her egg delivered into
some frenzied warbler's nest.
Sensing freedom quivering along her wing,
her mate calls out with unleashed joy in pitch-perfect C,
wuck-ooo wuck-oo wuck-oo, repeating his two-noted glee on and on ...
song streaming along lazy-beds of breeze,
as I am stopped, amazed to hear that singing for the first time –
unwooden and alive.

Death Dream

for a friend nearing her death

From the heat of Fiji I call you,
spilling with tales of bright fish, glory shells.
You gather it in to warm that Connemara house,
then lapse into silence.

Inside my dreaming sleep
edges are ragged along the high cliff road,
ocean spread wide below
and far out, all shark-skin-blue.

He is driving, but who knows why?
It must be a journey to somewhere
and I am content with it, not restless,
with the winding road and the view there.

Suddenly, a fall of rain over the ocean.
Not the whole sky raining, just this sheaf,
thick veil of wet beads halfway out,
a cascade water-falling from sky into sea.

Below, a whirlpool is beginning,
spinning round, around, and then forward,
drops whiten into fig-shaped pearls,
moon's alabaster tears.

They become rents, shredding sections of
tumbling fabric through which, inside or behind them,
light glows, daisy-white, bright as a fat moon
naked and full in the pupil-dark.

'So lovely,' I say stunned by it, as we drive into bends,
'so astonishing,' I breathe, 'you won't believe this!'
'Should we pull over?' he asks
angling the car toward a wide edge.

Instantly, it crumbles, disappears, wheels rolling over,
and he is saying, 'I'm so sorry, I'm so sorry!'
I lie down along the front seat, head against his leg,
waiting for the terror, the drop, the scarlet smash.

But it never comes.
We glide out into that brilliance,
that unbroken light now above the sea,
moving through no barrier

dissolving with unhurried calm
going smoothly into its radiance
as if that torn veil simply opens,
as if sails of rain have caught us up, into the drift of light.

Sailing to Cong along the N59

for Eileen Keane

It's blowing hard.
Water cascading down the Bens' bare bones
is spume on the ocean,
fingers of it stretched across their stone rumps;
it's steam from the fat funnel of an old tug
struggling in a storm.
The road is a slipstream I'm shooting,
white line just a vague border to cross and
recross in the glide.
Exciting,
                              frightening.
Up to Maam the grasses are old-gold, rose-gold
and swept flat by force, juddering upright in the breaks,
but after Corr na Móna avenues of tall plane trees
shake leaves free, spiralling across the road tight as a tune,
then, ungrasped, lost and foundering
spin out across Joyce's loughs.
It doesn't matter.
The yellow and red glee of their flight was worth it.

But I'm following the rainbow.
Out of torrential rods of grey,
sun has suddenly cleared the sky of cloud
so that purple, pink and green can ribbon the earth,
a great thread round the perfect gift,

and I'm chasing it with no desire,
no need to get over it to the other side,
simply to follow along, mouth open in awe,
until here it stops at Cong with you
on your fiftieth birthday, showering Lisloughrey Lodge with
a swatch of colour in that sudden clarity of an autumn day.
How difficult it was to get this far,
how easy to go on.

II   UNBROKEN STONE IN A STUBBORN SEA

Unbroken Stone in a Stubborn Sea
– Epic of Inishbofin

for Máire O'Halloran, and for Aidan

You sit beneath lamplight, Máire, pensive at dusk,
alabaster skin sky-smooth, flapper-bob dark as winter midnight
falling round your pearls, a string of harvest moons that light your smile.
This is written for you. Because you love this island,
because Irish still lives in the shape of your lips
and history is your comfort on a cold night, books floating
in your curled lap while currents run vagrant on *Trá Gheal*.

One of twelve, your husband's father Michael became a teacher,
sent off-island to college. His father, Martin, was a fisherman
from Inishark, small island of shale and slate, hunkering a few short miles
of capricious sea from Bofin. The last families were taken off in 1960.
Where the light of memory would flit among the houses,
oyster catchers and gannets now wheel through bare rafters, ribs only left
of homes that once shook with laughter, or with grief as the boats went down.

Stories wintering in him like seed, Martin knew how rough the hands,
how split with salt, island living made them, as it carved itself into their skins,
and a life lived elsewhere might never break a man like the sea.
Better ink to trace the fine outline of a hand, better the dust of chalk
with solid boards beneath the feet, than brine-filled lungs in the sea's work.
Books might take you further than the shore or the wild bondage of an island's rim.

Island people learned to read the weather.
Not a gift like stone-walling or the sight, but necessity, instinct,
as a bird might need to find its path home.
Sea, sky, a swish of seals – that's what eyes were keen for.
Bad weather starts at the bottom of the sea,
too much weed in the nets foretells storms,
shoals of fish slapping the hard face of the surface, signal wind.

Martin knew about survival by the way clouds were
laid out on a bed of sky, the peel of chiming waves
off the rocks at an edge of Bofin, and watching *Leac a' Tairbh*
a bull neck of rock at the end of Shark
on which the ocean swell paints the shape of a ship in salt.
If it sails seaward, weather will be good –
but if it's returning, sailor beware.

Little warning in a fine day though – great lump of sea
suddenly rising, storm funnelling out of nowhere,
gathering the waters into itself, drawing them higher, higher,
boat a splinter on the mountain's rump,
then shaken off and 'falling, falling down for half-an-hour'
to find its level on the hard shoulder of sea,
smashed men tangled in their nets, everything drowned but screams.

Too harsh on Shark and Bofin, all the losses.
A life might sink under their weight were it a row-boat
like those overloaded with seaweed or fish, men slipping
into their places in the drowning racks below,
an anchorage reserved for them under Atlantic swells.
Pulling a man from the waves was madness –
meant taking his place – they knew that.

St Colman's churchyard sprouts a list in stone of fishermen
drowned from Bofin. Mary Darcy lost two husbands that way
and two sons. Names like Tierney, Connolly, Lavelle,
O'Toole and Scuttle recur, trailing children and brothers in their wake.
It grew so long that list, a new plaque beneath
John Behan's celtic cross weeping its brass-green tears
says simply – to 'all those who lost their lives at sea.'

Three Lacey men from Shark, on Bofin for mass and a pint,
lost off *Trá Geal*, had beached their boat on the shifting sands
of the golden smile where families bake in the sun.
But the spiral there of the rip below, only needed one
unsteady boat to pull towards the wrack and deeper weed,
speedy currents a ready drag. Oars and rudder were
tossed up on some distant shore, and one body.

You might be out to load herrings, mackerel, ling and gurnard
off the Bofin Bank boiling with white fish tails
thrusting into rainbows. Ten thousand would fish the world's
finest fishing grounds in 1880. A battle for local men –
fifteen hundred islanders in row-boats against
ten thousand in ships with sail, the catch
slipping away to Germany, the Shetlands, America.

You might be after Basking Sharks feeding on plankton
and sunshine close to the sea's skin on the Sunfish Bank
thirty miles off Erris Head. Rowboats were never
a match for a fish thirty-six feet long and a rapid swimmer.
Six men took three hours of rowing
to catch up with it, pulling in quietly
so the keenest eye, steadiest arm could harpoon the beast.

Once speared it dived deep uncurling seventy fathoms of line,
dragging the boat behind it past miles, till exhausted
it was pulled up, one man leaping onto its back to slice out the liver.
That oil brought fifty pounds in the 1830's
when renting one acre cost five shillings to the landlord.
Hoarded, it was back-up when storms made fields the only food.
All the lamps would blaze that night, if the boat came home.

You could be lucky – go back to the house for a sweater
like John Moran, boat leaving without you, or survive one storm
to die in another, or simply be following those fish with their slinky tails
flashing rainbows across the white spume above the breakers
when the storm strikes in '27,
killing forty-five from island and coast,
ending driftnet fishing in the rowboats of Bofin.

You might be two young students in '76 from the prairies of Kansas
where the sky was their sea – boundless blue, deep with air, tideless.
Adventure a slick of shining in their eyes,
they knew nothing of salty rips. Climbing The Stags –
antlers of rock reaching toward heaven – limbs taut in the
unconquerable strength of youth, they watched the tide cut them off.
A huge thing the sea, growing bigger, wider, churning up panic.

The space across seemed short enough. They plunged in,
waves swallowing them whole, squeezing breath from them.
John Behan's lattice of iron cross now gazes at the spot,
a mosaic of air and iron you can see the whole big sky through.
Walking with Alex and Brendan you might see seals clotted on rocks,
curved head and tail pointing towards the sky in mimicry of a half moon,
just once hear them moaning, strange, deep, in an odd rough keening.

There was no gift missing on this island – musicians, poets,
fishermen, blacksmiths, tailors
dressmakers, cobblers, weavers, and healers.
Old cures sent bodies strongly onto the sea's crest –
cobwebs would staunch a bleed, boiled nettles still a cough,
garlic crush colds, and mouldy bread was saved
for cuts and wounds, penicillin still beyond make-believe.

A place where poets came to rest from their Darkness,
questing the western light. The madness of Theodore Roethke
burned here, his lovely quotation on the walls of Day's bar,
long narratives from Richard Murphy arrived, as alive and flowing
as air currents that filled his canvas as he spun around the islands
in his old Galway Hooker 'Ave Maria', sailing a quarrelling
Sylvia Plath with Ted Hughes to Bofin from the Pier Bar in Cleggan.

An island so loaded with fairies – their stories written out by Francesca Wilde
before she advised Oscar to stand his ground – their breath still fills
Gap na Siog, the Fairy Gap, the fairy fort *Lois* in Middlequarter Mount,
the fairy rock *Caisleån a Tulác*, the fairy cliff *Aill a' Phuca*.
Such a small island for such a big history, a name for every inch of land,
rock and lough, written into the black bog, the cliff forts,
a place older than long ago when bronze was just an imagined gleam.

St Colman made his radical swerve here away from Rome, his disgruntled
English monks finally sent to Mayo, illuminated scripts abandoned
beside the need for farming by the Irish brothers who remained.
Cromwell stole the old church stone by stone crushing everything catholic,
built his star-shaped fortress at the harbour mouth mixed with blocks from
Gránuaile's castle, locking sacrilege onto the rocks
when Bofin, last stronghold to surrender, in 1623 became a prison.

Priests were murdered, their 'high treason' soaking into fields of blood,
or shackled to the Bishop's Rock, left to drown as the tide rose.
Many joined woman, man and child sent as slaves to Barbados
among the fifty thousand a year his soldiers shipped out.
And they broke language out of those left, children with sticks
hung round their necks, notched each time their tongue
curled round Irish, the tally mounting towards punishment.

And they took the boats. And the right of an Irish man to own one.

Today the harbour catches the traveller looking for safe tide.
No-one needs to learn to read the waters, nor do they see in pre-dawn,
waves shot-silk, oars loaded with phosphorous – the 'eye of the sea' –
watching. The old family cottage is larger – re-roofed,
re-painted, re-claimed. Windows once small to avoid the English
window tax, open wide, gathering light into the house
that gazes seaward across a garden torn up by sheep.

Drowning, famine, cholera – TB, slavery and war –
the harsh life of the fisherman, the struggles of his wife –
comfort is built out of these on this Island of the White Cow.
Your children come and go, building their separate paths.
You have stitched it in with family thread –
the land, the sea, this sky you gaze on now
late light washing it purple. Their island marrow is rich with it.

I watch you across the fire, reading. You make the crossing each chance you have,
holding the place close, reshaping what might have been lost if tides of knowledge
had swept your husband too far east, too far for returning.
We walk the greening hills in all weathers, or the track through bog black as coal
holding a sheep's sightless skull, or rough roads where sea-pinks spring wiry
out of stone fences, clumps of St Patrick's Cabbage with their swollen leaves,
clusters of samphire, green, succulent, resisting the salt-thrashing winter brought.

Your father loved the sea so much he travelled to the coast
when he heard the whisper of death, grew you up with salt in your veins,
languages in your mouth and islands in your bones.
You are not from here. You grew into it, stone by stone, plant by plant.
You knotted with it through marriage, through your longing,
and your soul sings here, knowing as many do
that home is not always the place your birth gives you.

III CHANGING TIDES

Mourning

Dusk is falling like dust into the air,
day creeping away with the light.
Through trees that block out blue
I stumble down into the valley
feet squelching on the track
sliding into dark undergrowth.

And then the lake.
A bird high up sits in its mirror tree
rustling branches, chasing nectar,
yet the water's face remains still, totally
unmarked in its reflection, ripples
impossible under the weight of sky on its skin.

Standing in knee-high grass on the edge,
water lilies are blank green cards,
flowers not yet roused into certainty.
An owl hoots, so close
its breath seems to rustle against my nape
and it begins in synchrony – my own deep call –

vibrating a thrum in the chest, a fluttering wind
trapped in the throat, a growing howl in the cave of mouth,
erupting low and guttural, then rising in flight,
pooling into the dome of tree-tops,
a voice keening into sobs the damp face of forest receives,
without grief or sorrow, and remains untouched.

Shaping the Dark

three readings of Tony Lloyd's oil on linen painting 'On a dark night you can see forever'.

Day is so cluttered with definition:
angles of buildings, aqua pools in backyards,
powerlines, and the fraught confusion of clouds.
The night's black velvet though –
unwritten upon, still opening ahead –
could be any time, any place.

**

i. Night is soft as longing.
This road so lean, like her body,
limbs ivory as the lines on it,
smooth and sinuous as the trunks of trees
shed of bark, dancing in the headlights,
and her eyes brighter than the city glitter below.
When you meet at the top of the high mount
all the world splayed out below,
she will tell you this is forever,
that all this could be yours.
Your heart accelerates with the drive up,
a small planet bouncing against your ribs,
and you ache for the holding of her,
sable hair blocking out the moon.
In the dark anything seems possible.
Winding the window down, trees are slowly shivering.
A leafy rustling in the illicit shadow is whispering:
'why are you here?'

**

ii. Night holds history inside its black cape.
You know when your unit reaches the top of this ridge
your truck will turn, unload, and the firing begins.
Sarajevo sits sparkling, a diamond sunk below the ring of hills,
cosmopolitan, blended Ottoman and Austrian and Bosnian,
a jangle of colour, a tight woven history.
You enjoy the lights now – 'like fairyland' your mother used to say –
and she'd wonder now 'what are you doing here?'
People below don't know what you know.
That they are targets, ducks in a shooting gallery.
That fifteen hundred children will be killed, ten thousand adults.
Three hundred mortars a day will burn their books, crush their history,
buildings ashed, bodies dismembered.
For four years – no heat, no power, no water, no food.
Then they will know blackness –
a lightless city where only your flares will ignite it
so mortars can find victims in the dimness.

                    **

iii. Night is full of fairytales, those lights below stunning.
Still, it's just the drive home, nothing special.
Ordinary, you suppose. That's what life is after all.
This moment captured in your heart, the road winding up
and the rattling city beneath a furry moon. Good to leave it.
Lovely, yes, to live up here above the stars below,
to feel the kids have trees to breathe in
and a deep mist swirling on sunrise.
Then the whole world's pink and hazy.
You'd think this road goes on forever
but it doesn't.
It stops at your house, with the fire lit,
kids in pyjamas, their Dad tired
but happy with his day's painting,
waiting for the last piece of that puzzle – you –
to slide in out of the dark,
lighting the front path home.

Night Watch

Time is elastic, its zenith fit to breaking
when you wait for the ambulance – now leaning over him,
now rushing back and forth from house to street straining
for sirens, night so dark and wet and quiet out there.

Listening for breath in a slight boy of fifteen years
is an ancient art requiring silence. Kneeling on your hall floor,
ear right to his lips, beside the frenzied shouts of his father,
whose panic of pacing is the only thing he can offer him.

Your own son watches his friend from the corner,
slumped, slightly beaten, the first fire of alcohol seeming
less necessary than it might have been, not worth the effort now,
while the friend he tried to carry home lies on his side, still.

Slapping his rump to try and wake him feels like assault.
Strange to be able to do things he would never allow,
ice you run across his cheeks a cruelty. Beyond limp,
he will not jerk away, open his mud-brown eyes.

When they finally come, wearied knights of the new wars,
they cannot rouse him, tell us it's not good, open his lids to pupils
so huge, so pitch and utterly void, his mother gasps, sinking,
and you never saw anyone so unconscious who wasn't dead.

You make your son sit and watch. They strap on an oxygen mask,
fail to open his mouth for a tongue block, quietly ask what he took –
vodka yes, but weed? pills? needles? No. Just vodka. Straight.
'He was kicked,' your boy says, 'they punched me in the head.' And vomits.

Clipped on a stretcher, they lift him out of the hall. In the long night,
fourteen hours twisted in tubes before he rouses, you remember
they loved pizza by the swimming pool for the last three birthdays, watched
videos, Xbox, played Star Wars with Darth Vader the only enemy –

and when you turned sixteen no-one had parties at all.

Brief Sport

You see her from the highway
where the tall eucalypt stands greyly at the edge of bush,
dumb with its necklace of flowers,
drooping as if it, too, is weary of the weight.
She leans as if to kneel,
caught into the slump of her mute grief,
careless in the tangle of her clothes
at the end of the long thread of skid.
Its burn of rubber, odourless now,
scars an uncomprehending earth
right to the tree's roots,
black scores against the young,
their sport cut short.

Across this broad land, strings of floral crosses
tacked on trees, guard rails, signposts,
sprout names in a tortured kind of style,
road maps tagged out by a new form of headstone.
Dot-to-dot drawing pages from the book of youth,
they link them in migration points under their flight
towards that un-aged land where years evaporate in a blaze.
She laces the trunk with fresh flowers,
blooms left yesterday wilting in the sear of summer heat.
Winter will never arrive with its resting dark,
her son already days behind in history, just
a photo on the mantle, heat-welded to his eighteenth year.

As We that are Left

for Robert Gray

It glided into my half-waking,
clock still with hands too far from the bell,
and time was on my mind again,
and I could hear your voice,
older on the phone and warm, saying
'I remember you, you know.'

And it surprised, took away easy speech, brought
waves up from the well of a certain kind of loneliness.

Life has epochs that seem as large
as all those measurements of dinosaurs,
and the stories are fossils
buried until another quake breaks open layers
or pushes one through another,
confusing remnants
so dating them becomes a science.

I kept moving, and every decade the faces changed and
I thought it wasn't important because I was used to people
forgetting. It seemed right, the nature of things.

But I remember you too
and all the others, all you handsome men,
and the rough timber table in John's house
and Bob's eyes and Rae's hands
and the women round the table, mostly quiet then.

I wonder what you remember – a young woman,
shyness mixed with outrage at everything,
a resistance to being boxed, even by the new 'freedom'?
It was hard being a woman then.
The sky was only a wedge of blue.

What I remember most were
words
and the ways of entering you took into the air around you

and the land, and the sky and the trees;
the way they made everything more merged.

Sometimes I feel like I've been a wraith all my life,
a transparency that slipped across a moment
and was gone into the next;
that I never fixed myself anywhere but
slid across the memories of others, just a shiver.

I so wanted to ask you last night:
'What? What do you remember; and when?
Who was I? Who was there, did we laugh and was I
happy and why, why remember?'

But I hugged it to me that instant and was silent,
phone too modern for cradling, and in the later dark
I thought you could be mistaken after more than thirty years
and it was some other girl you recalled and
if I asked I'd know by your tone of voice
or the tale itself you'd tell, that I was
never there that moment you thought of.
And I didn't want to hear that, at all.

The Space You Inhabit

i.m. Jacob Rosenberg 1922 – 2008

You said that poetry remembers
where history forgets itself.
You told me, words have shadows
left behind after they pass the lips.
You gave me your poem, 'The Little Boat',
its simplicity, its tenderness,
the song of its longing drift and faraway port.

Vivid, your eyes with a child's sparkle.
Tough, your judgement with a parent's certainty.
A good age when we met, your generous heart
held the map of a painful knowledge.
And your forgiveness – escapee from a hatred
incomparable, systematic, premeditated – still named
the lesson we should carve into our souls for vigilance.

But this life of yours –
what celebration of compassion, what creativity.
How did camps exterminate so much
yet leave you with a voice?
How did horror so express its hieroglyphics of loathing,
yet leave you with language a breeze in your sails?
Robbed of family, you clung to the steerage of imagination.

Out of traditions of prayer and chant,
out of a history of learning and burning,
your mind anchored itself in stone, rock, sweat.
From the school of the ghetto, university of Auschwitz,
and in the belly of Mauthausen tagged 'return not desired',
moment by moment, you lifted the boulder, counted the steps,
all the while gathering timbers in your mind
to frame your small craft, furling canvas for its voyage.

Solid in the very air, smoke its ink, screams its text,
a murderous wave rolled across Europe.
And yet after, the Little Boat, buoyant, bobbing, carried
you at the helm, breathing in the clean sea-salted air.
You drew from the heave and list, the wisdom to know
how to leave the word and its shadow with us.

Regret only for time's speed, lost moments,
their waste fills my mourning, your spirit
skimming from moorage across the last open tide.
I hold onto the poems you left
between the covers of a book
whose frame will one day crumble.
But you? Not as long as poetry remembers.

No End to Voyaging – Reading *Nine Bright Shiners*

for Theo Dorgan, in thanks

That's the time to read poetry,
at 2.00 am, the body present to pain,
waiting for pills to ease it off
where they once flung back my arm,
twisted ribs that still stick,
to carve out the bulb in my breast.
And I don't mind. I get to live.

That's the time to read poetry,
at 2.30 am, walking among your dead.
So many, Theo, so many sets of bright eyes
from winters old, from summers young,
their laughter, their lost time.
You have peopled my dark with them,
shining stars in a new constellation.

That's the time to read poetry,
at 2.45 am, when I know for certain this aloneness
has always been my path, settled into it,
marvelling how your own solitude had
fallen away into love long ago and its
spring truth, that those hands will
hold yours all the way home.

That's the time to read poetry,
at 3.00 am, Atlantic gale whistling
where the window-seal failed, moon
struggling against it towards full, chimney booming,
fearing for my father, my friend, a wild world away,
older for the first time at 94 and after, I
imagine, my slow lonely road ahead.

That's the time to read poetry though,
at 3.30 am, wearied, worn by worry, frayed
by the trapped knife working the ribs,
dawn still a way off, warmly crowded by love in your poems,
suddenly grateful, and sure because of you this minute –
of what it is we hold onto, hold on for –
words – sweet words – and their tender breath.

Legacy

I have seen these men,
going steadily about their business,
some raising their children carefully
with, like you, the quiet, exhausted,
ragged intent of women,
caressing without smothering
directing without force.
I have known them, in you,
kind and whimsical as a lover,
no thrusting presumption
behind an endless blue of the open eye.

I have seen them lost too,
hungry for the gaze of desire –
the body that needs too many eyes to admire it,
heart that recruits too many women to fill it –
helpless boy still wandering inside
eager for abiding care,
hungry for safe love,
ripped from a childhood
ruptured and torn by your own father.

Five years old and woken in fright
from the float of sleep
by his frictional rubbing weight,
heavier than his body on yours,
denser than the black night,
more piercing into manhood than even
the screams of a small boy
striating the slumbering house
again and again
year on year
falling into the deaf well of the dark.

Pain and its memory cut you off from closeness,
fear sheaths your open heart.
In the foggy drugged alleys of night
you search for burial sites,
while a gentle loving of yourself
remains a dream.

And those who love you, like I,
wait on the borderlands of trust,
while in nursery-rhyme rhythm your mantra,
over and over tolls at the gateway:

'I know what you don't know
and all my life I'll understand –
love conceals invasion, sweetheart,
trust lies buried in fear.
Daddy made me special, darling –
Daddy made me … dear.'

Puffing Smoke?

People are buying-up in the funeral business.
They're getting ready for the baby-boomers.
It'll be boom all right.

Debates are emerging on the carbon footprint of
coffin versus cremation and the bad news is,
cremation is four times the CO_2 of burial.

But then you have to take into account
the mowing of graves.
That brings it down a bit, relative-like.

We could go the way of freezing them,
then shatter the body to oblivion.
No footprint there.

We can make warm alkaline baths,
pretend it's like 're-entering the womb, man,'
and dissolve them, all these boomers.

What were their parents *thinking*!?
Post-war replacements, or thank god you're back,
or, my god, sex again, and again, and again?

New biodegradable sheaths are available instead of coffins.
Do-it-yourself backyard jobs are back on the list.
Cheaper. Kerry Packer did it that way. And he was rich.

With the greenhouse awareness level rising,
rules are really going to change.
You can feel it in the air.

No-one wants to be forgotten.
But no-one wants their footprints to be
that much bigger than their boots.

Changing Weather

She always goes.
She's used to it,
the blue-moon nature of seasonal loving.
Once a year, thick on her lips,
blackberry-rich
his red wine fuels
music riding her veins,
poems fingering her heart.
That's the best part.

And then, there's the crumpled bed,
crumbs from salted avocado on toast,
crushed pepper, lemon zest,
juice from a pomegranate his hands have rolled
staining her mouth,
spiced cherries tasting of Marrakech –
everything he makes speaking of his attention
to things, his attention.

Now, there would be too many in the bed.
Real love, stepping light inside a fresh breath,
enters his home fluid as change,
undarkening each corner
under that welcome gaze.
And in her own house with its tidal shades,
somewhere at the back
a door quietly closing.

Outdwellers

Torquay, Victoria

Isthmus: a narrow strip of land connecting two land masses.
Isthmus: a narrow passage connecting two cavities.

Once it protected Lisbon, Tower of Belém,
sitting far out in the River Tagus.
Moorish battlements over ribs of bulwark naves,
gun breaches filled with canon
facing all four corners of the earth.
They were nine and eleven, the cabin boys sailing with
Vasco da Gama's fleet, heading into open water
fearful they might be sailing off the edge of the world.

They were seven and nine, my sons straddling the parapets.
They saw the maps on the walls,
countries designated by strange animals,
rhinos, elephants, tigers, lions.
'Imagine,' he said, 'the first time you saw one and you were just a kid.'
'Imagine,' I said, 'not coming home until you were 11 years old!
And Vasco da Gama grew up in a seaside village like you.'
'And he was an adventurer, Mum, exploring the whole world! Like us.'

It was 2000, the year of change.
By then the Tower had lost its independence
linked by an isthmus of sand to the bank,
river so silted we could walk it.
'It was more exciting once wasn't it, Mummy
when it was far out in the river,
an island, with its own life, and ships?' he said. 'Yes.'

Corridor: thin strip of land allowing access
Corridor: restricted pathway for a particular mission
Corridor: literally, a place for running.

That Tower. My town –
once an island, a village by the sea,
cut off from the metropolis,
the road in, a single lane surrounded by trees.
City people really had to *travel* here.
I chose it because it reminded me of Shellharbour,
the town I grew up in, on a hill overlooking the sea,
unsealed road the pathway home, as it once was here.

There too, farms bordered the town.
Thick with cows, you could hear them
grumbling at early milking,
sea rumbling pebbles on the beach below.
Sold up. All around now.
Just a tsunami of brick as it rushes toward town,
tumbling over flower farms,
scraping the earth clear of everything green,
concrete beds stuck on skeletal land.
We're the 'growth corridor' now –
or the end of it.

Winter's Last Crush

from Clochán, the house of Iris and Michael, Errislannan

The sparrow hawk at Iris and Michael's is diving for mice,
pickings sparse at the tail-end of a brutal winter,
field below all mountain grass, brown and frost-dead.
Everything green on the earth has been driven underground.
Iris sees the sun and moon dipping and rising in unison
a set of scales caught in their search for balance.

In Roundstone Pottery where Seamus spins clay into shape,
Rose paints porcelain ringed with dark-cobalt fish, sea-women in weed
trailing the rims, or a flutter of flowers green and blue as if sea-drowned.
Still, their mermaid's escape from the dark ice of winter is a surprising
potter's trick, a swish of navy-grey tail sliding off the window ledge
at *Clochán*, disappearing into an imagined deep.

Below, sea-wings of deep swell hide a bay full of dolphins.
Ash from a volcano in Iceland is coming in with the salt.
A woman is disappearing off Mannin rocks
trying to scatter her sister's ashes.
Just the one wave, always in the Irish West, just the one.
And the earth is frozen a foot down.

Everywhere along the peninsula winter is white-hard,
sea itself frozen around the bay. Michael's garden is ice-burnt black.
Dock has rusted into fragments, potatoes wilted back into the dark peat.
Salt gales wrap themselves round tomato and bean shoots
strangling their green, while fuchsia hedges are sliced
clean of every leaf by gales of barbed-wire whips.

Hard to believe the sticks still left will return us their scarlet
and purple flowers weeping onto the track next year.
That stems of orchids like crocus will blaze violet,
each petal a flower opening its mouth, tongue reaching for summer sky.
Lilac heavens at 11pm will soften our waters to a shimmering
over-polished pewter, or the blue of vein through young skin.

But not now. Spring warmth is still a shadowy past.
This is the closing of a cold-scorched season
struggling with aftershocks, an early spring of fire-gazing indoors,
watching the howling force crust my front windows with sea-sweat.
It clings like sheets of ice, salt-ponds, rippled and crazed,
and the mist crusting the lights into frozen stars.

Three Poems for Susan

i.m. Susan Gallagher, Ireland 1942 – 2007

1 Beside the Glass Wall

Tonight, that comes in earlier each day
bringing the edge of winter on its breath,
the moon rose just off full, red from the sea
trembling a little as heron-blue clouds
dabbed at it, dried it white.
I knew a shift in these clouds
was like the shuffle of things the day you died.

When a friend dies, everything is
thrown unsteady as the
weightless dust of their leaving
unbalances the axis of earth
slightly, for the moment.
Small shock-ripples
tremble along the edge of being;
some simple essence
that has to renew itself,
reform in a different shape,
absorbing the space that was once filled.

When it comes back to itself,
solid and real as the trees in this forest,
it is new fabric out of the old,
re-shuttled and whole, its warp and weave
a little jagged where the absence is mended,
a little less perfect, a little more frayed
beneath the texture of skin.
Perhaps in its fathomless nature,
there is spirit made more wise
for the human failings it inherits
from the moment it passed through as human flesh.

Others may barely notice,
but we who are left, we see it –
the fall of the body into dust,
its caving inwards,
a charcoal trace that holds the after-image,
a shiver of outline
surrounding what was full and rich and lively
before erasure, centre vacant now.
There is a resettling of all living things.
There is a sadness tucked into the hem of being.
There is, certainly, a beginning again.

2 Blue Moon
on *a Month's Mind*

Here is the last night of June – blue moon here –
though where you were it came in May,
a glow at the end of your final sigh.
Month's Mind spins across the world in emails,
stories are whirling turnstiles.
Rituals have been performed, cremation,
ashes scattered in two countries.

I read your texts still captured in my phone,
emails bound into my hard drive.
Best is your radio voice on disc
that wet Letterfrack day you talked
poetry with me on air.
But you are so totally absent.
All I have are objects – the sand woman sculpture,

scarves, your poems, the artwork you helped my son make
out of burned chocolate wrappers, wool and paint
still on his father's fridge door –
things we collected, created, exchanged,
photographs, and a history only two knew –
all the lovely detritus of shared moments of living
sweeter than hot blackberries we picked one summer.

We were adventurers, you and I,
splicing ourselves into Connemara's shores,
tunnelling into its dark brown heart in the west bogs
to find riches of belief and practice
that help the soul bind itself
to all good things – music, poems, the land.

Outsiders searching, we learned that spirit
lies close to the surface in Ireland,
it can't be forgotten or lost,
soaked deep into bones and stones,
tingling in fingertips on fiddle and pipes,
rolled round an accent
none but home-grown Irish can master.

Being seed blown back from generations lost, we knew
leavings are our habit – we can do them in the dark –
that returning is what we only half-know in the body,
carried in our genes like a tune often hummed
a part-recalled melody searching for its words
elusive except on the tip of the tongue,
or the cusp of a dream that could be memory.

Being returners, we sensed that belonging
is to be earned in a silent waiting way,
carried in the misty air, on damp smiling faces
nodding recognition on a late night walk
along a road familiar as skin,
heaven the only light needed, stars glancing off a boat's rollick,
wet rocks a sky-mirror along the bay of the low road.

You were fading. I visited. I took you home. I left.
Each day after, we talked across oceans.
I only saw your sunflower face in photos,
growing more golden than gorse, than wild yellow Iris.
Your breath became the measure of how close you were
to light's horizon as certainty grew that your readiness
made death another journey to be yearned for.

You called me guide, teacher of the heart,
but I knew lessons were exchanged, and
what guide becomes lost like this
in the death of a friend?
You feel so utterly gone from me,
how can I hold onto the light, belief in anything?
Meditation brings me only the knowledge that 'we can't understand'.

If there were only something more than 'no-thing'.
This mourning month I have forgotten too much,
wailed into the forest, raged at the sea,
broke my heart among the ashes of the long-dead
knowing they only remain because they live inside me,
will pass into the forgotten at my death,
and in turn, my own small life fall invisible, erased.

3 Formlessness

You died in a day I had already passed through.
What exact hour, on which exact day?
I struggle to get it right, mind urgent,
as if it is important –
a peg on the climb up a cliff's haggard face
or a stake in the heart of death.
Yet, here is the silence
and you are nowhere.
The small self struggles.
Can we be more than this?

Words are a mist on the shore
clouding the ocean, vacant wrappers
in which we cannot capture death
nor memory hold life back from it.
Rainforest here is washed clean today.
Still, leaf cannot capture the rain
that thunders and then is gone.
Air cannot hold onto the wave's roar
nor beach-sand remain the same,
imprint of current washed away.

Beyond the barrier of shore
ocean fills into waves that
return to the unfettered sea.
And so much water, we reduce to dew,
or as dust, ash, return to the finite soil.
Molten as glass we unshape.
Complex as love we unravel.
Is it then the true one within
becomes itself again infinite, irreducible,
suspended in a greater formlessness of soul?

Benediction

breast cancer check, Melbourne, 2006, 2012, 2014

Stillness spills from a sleet-white sky
this unpeopled Monday, absence
taking advantage before a public holiday.

Streets are bare, and the casual among us
sit a moment in Fitzroy Gardens
with coffee and brandy snap.

Quiet lies in the branched web of old trees,
huge, just standing, the day unremarkable,
neither dull nor bright.

Solicitude levitates in pea-green grass
too lush for this drought.
Someone has been caring.

In the hospital behind, films record their staccato serial,
ten then sixteen-years of pictures – two breasts, one healed
of cancer, though scars rivet the trudge toward fragile ribs.

A good day. My children far away, safe home,
wait for my return by dark,
more than a decade since they were five and two.

Memory is worth its role of attending to the past,
so that in the present, thankfulness brims in the eye,
blurring a terrible tenderness in the green air.

Known by Heart

Her skin chronicles his touch throughout the years – hands long-fingered, strong and
vellum-soft, once unspotted by age. Luminous, they held her face,
tracing that forbidden pathway in the dark under his Abbey walls.

Tender with longing – restraint – they picked for her that wild pink rose,
walking above the Glen of Aherlow twelve years into a longer good-bye.

They gestured like fluttering doves, pointing out a white swan
nesting on a lake's island, a grey heron beside it
watching, guarding – two companions so unmatched.

Hands praying a lifetime of prayer, bound his body into the swaddling
of surplice, delivered wine and wafer, married others together for life.

Years pass faster than water runs across her wrist. Yet still his fingers
always twist his greying hair as he talks, eyes of lightning-blue glance in
mock-teasing, and her heart flinches to find these simple things still endear.

After thirteen years those palms held her naked, trembling, a skin-magic
love makes, burning along the abiding thread that holds her to him.

Impossibly out of time – love like that. Slowly his hands grew older
practised in rituals of denial. Awaiting surgery their ligaments contracted
to a right-hand claw, placid, white-cold as he cast her adrift.

Or so it seemed. Though never certain of the unattainable they wanted,
caged by rules that never concerned her, they were life to him, chosen, re-chosen.

And yet – meeting thirty years on, his grasp is warm in celebration, that
split from each other as the times demanded, they can still walk
Coole Park together, sharing the stroke of trees shady-green along their lips.

Bright Moment

for Subhana Barzaghi Roshi, after her poems

Inside,
this room is black
as the shade in onyx.
But outside the window
full moon is ripe, swelling radiance,
its blown light pushing round
edges of the blind.

Its breath
soft and full of white
is puffing the window shade
inward,
then drops back,
as if like wind it were
sighing through the cracks.

Rise.
Reach out fingers to
curl around the
tassel spilling like silk,
falling,
falling from the hard edge of board.

Simply lift it. Let go.

Washed away,
          interior night;
drowned,
          all dark mind;
dazzling,
          this flooded ancient ground.

IV ALONG THE DRIFT

Afterword

i.m. Seamus Heaney, 13 April 1939 – 30 August 2013

It was the week after your funeral mass.
Your poem 'Postscript' was meandering through me,
with your 'government of the tongue', your message about voice,
unique sound of a poet come into themselves.
I was re-arriving, driving from Clifden,
the road you knew well, out
along the marbled spine of our peninsula,
jetlagged, 'neither here nor there'.
Packed overgrowth from summer was so full
compared to the stark cold spring I left earlier in the year,
when you were reading and writing, knowing already
tomorrows are best left uncounted.
It was a soft day but no wind to blow the dust off a long trip,
no hurry in the low-slung sky,
a slight hush in the lightly wet wheels.

Air had been thoroughly soaked and a
county-full of spiders busy at work.
The land was hung as if for Christmas –
every tip of gorse branch, each dip of lavender heath,
every vacant space between the cups of fuchsia,
was glitter-strung. Thousands of webs, millions of drops,
netted a tinselled land, branches rising
as shimmering limbs from the bog,
or perhaps heaven had laid out a lacy crystal cloth
that angels at play dropped careless beneath long hugging clouds,
and the trees, reaching up, had torn it about themselves
in bliss at their lovely ornament.

Or maybe, for a small moment, the earth,
feeling aged beyond counting, had
webbed-over with wearied loss,
grown ancient at your death.

Love Poem for Ita

for Ita O'Donovan – and John Curran, Errislannan, married 1962

Wine in hand, sun striking against the last stones of light,
we sit, poetic friends, and you read me another poem, really a love poem
for a husband still handsome in his autumn years, though you can't see it –
'I can *never* write a *love* poem for him' you groan.

True – your poems may not speak of his strong brown hands
still knotted to the land here, nor that his step travelled
far from you for work when the children were young,
distant but never faltering in holding you.

They don't tell that he was raised with another twelve in a family
locked into small measures – a room with an earthen floor,
flour bags for sheets, that before school he walked from Spiddal to Galway
before light unlocked the roads, donkey his only guide in the tar-black
dark at 4 am, turf and potatoes a market-bargain with tomorrow.

He spoke only Irish till secondary school when English
broke across his tongue roughly, a language for the way out –
and education, his mother said.
Now he tells his children in the 'new Ireland', and his grandchildren –
but they don't want to know, the same way I can't bear to
think of my father going to school with no shoes in winter.

These things are not in the way of a poem *you* might write.
But there he is in so many guises – cutting you a stone garden-seat
against which to rest your tired back, digging you a well
for the time you might need water if the lough fails in his absence,
beside you at a wake, boat loaded with candles in the dark,
or jealous of your time with the boys of verse, asking, 'but –
does *Heaney* know *anything* about *lettuce?*!' *

He is laughing through the backlines of your own humour
looking up names of wrack and flower for you, remembering
a way of saying things that you carry into your lines.
His clever mind still thrums with politics and opinion.
I love to listen to him shred a government rotten with waste,
before he leaves for more work on his wall outside,
ideal companion to your outrage at church abuse.

What is it that makes a marriage so easy with teasing,
secure in respect and love, so sharing in knowledge,
so right in his building for you, your cooking for him,
you might feel that *doing* for the other was not enough to show it?
Rooms in your stone house you rebuilt from fallen walls, fit together
like there never *was* a puzzle, and you two, whether grown or
worked that way, seem balanced in the mystery of love long-lived,
only a rare few are gifted to share.

* from the poem *Birth Days* by Ita O'Donovan

The Poem: In Defence of Excess

But I want it to run on, spilt,
to look out of control,
to *lose the run of itself*
when really, it's just
a certain kind of drive or desire,
body urgent to burst or spill,
words weeping a little
to bring us together in an
act of public tenderness.

Why must I scrape it thin for you,
carve it to a marrow-slim waist,
discipline it to cleverness,
take the breath out of it,
tell the lungs, *don't breathe now*,
when I want breath inside these bars,
or a sigh or a sob?
I don't want it opaque, starved or strangled.

Why should I tighten the poem,
take the deco out, un-brocade it,
tidy up baroque flourish,
when all day long
everything I see is layer on layer of excess,
the ridiculous glory of peacock feathers,
a mackerel's opalescent skin?

Why should I bow to form that contains,
that chains up colour, dams the flow of my veins,
when rainbows sweep past in floating bubbles
blown down the Hippodrome in Istanbul,
crowd barrels full of turmeric, chilli, cayenne
in the Spice Market?

And stars –
> should they take back all their childish glitter –
> so overdone, so unnecessary,
> so many cluttering up the dark?

Research Statement for Creative Works to be Submitted for Peer Review

Melbourne University

You ask for ethereal mist along this evening's shore
in a framework of dialectic accuracy.
Or the peacock's opal sheen in early sun
as geometric equation. Prove to me,
you say, that a lifetime of observation
can be explained as research, or that the heart's
double-shadow-gaze as mother, daughter, sufferer,
self-muse, can be added up like beads on an abacus.

These are the things I do know – a poem is written out of flesh,
the immeasurable soul, the watcher in the heart.
It comes from gathering, the attention to a caught instant –
that man as he helps the old woman into a car
gently cupping his hand above her head, protective,
becomes definitional – becomes 'tenderness'.

Poetry is not something we *do* but something we *be*.
And the research in understanding history, archaeology,
social relations, intimacy and politics is impossible to
capture except to say 'here is the poem'.

I know that dreams sometimes open the poem whole,
a moment like nothing else except the self-gone-ness of sex
and if not written under that blaze of a lightning-filled sky
or the warm yellow bed-lamp, it evaporates back into
landscape on the borderline of conscious and unconscious, lost again.

That to sit and write the poem, the known self must be absent,
as only a fine silken thread of awareness draws a poem out of the veins.
That after moments, there are those long years of twitching the line,
waiting, years of fine-etching on the parchment page
until what we know to be true – that words sing –
is settled under the pen in a scrimshaw language flawed yet finished.

You ask me for research background, significance, contribution.
Look to the poems written on the death of a friend that console,
or the loneliness of the suicide we recognise, or the sadness of war
in a history of young Kamikaze men that was ignored.
Look where the breath of the reader sighs...
'Yes. I know this. It feels

just like that.'

Meditations on Moonlight

Silent Vipassana retreat, Sangsurya (Place of Light), Byron Bay, NSW

From the deck on this green mountain ridge
sky is emptying out on the distant horizon, losing day.
A milk-filled moon bulging full is perfectly round with glazed skin.
In a moment its light will splatter like flour through a sieve of cloud
over the ocean's purple plate. Five minutes waiting,
then a bare shoulder laced with violet, shrugs off gathering storms
to rise a second time above mottled waves.
Clear of confusion, this ascension is effortless.

We think that roar we hear is the sea –
but that is the sound of light
pouring across breaking waves,
streaming across the stones of our own dark.
Voice dissipates in cool night air. We enter silence.
The stroke of black ink speaks, the almost-hush
of the pen's tongue as it skids under
gentle pressure across the white void.

We will wrestle the days, often aching, wounded,
clotted with grief and anger and desire.
Or calm in the quiet heart 'just sitting'.
Just sitting with the breath, our metronome, our anchor.
At night alone we stand in the forest after showers,
hearing the grasshopper jump, wallaby
crack branches on the lower path,
stitching ourselves with lunar silk to joy.

Waxing and waning is a moon's nature.
Each night it grows smaller
pared away slowly as if sharing exhausts it.
Time will again bring its ripened wholeness.
But now, we're travelling on, or homeward,
and it's the draught of that illumination
goes with us inside, knowing –
returning is what the light does best.

Driving Back from Knockroe

In the blue dusk
I took the wet way home
from Ballinrobe,
above the islands in Lough Corrib –
Joyce's country –
rhododendrons blooming
magenta and mauve,
white-thorn blossom
heavy confetti on the road,
rain spilling out
blueing the asphalt
now a slick trail.
Past the towering Bens,
old grey faces turned up
toward the splashed sky,
tears down their
quartz-white cheeks,
joy in their stubble
of wispy bog-cotton.
Past gold gorse shattered across hills,
sheep slovenly on the road sides,
and the rain fell on quietly
in the mauve light.
One errant cloud
had slipped down,
and thread-bare, circled
the Bens' mid-drift in
a haze of muslin-mystery.
Almost there – the last road –
above Clifden harbour,
winding through tall green spring
and out along the high spine of
the last mile.

Nick's boat absent, leaves a flat
spot of sky-still water
while he heads out toward the Azores.
From the end of our road, the Atlantic's edge,
a light embery-orange turns gold
beyond which mystery lies –
home just this side of the dark.

End of the Road

There's a cold corner at the end of the lane
where the heart of a house was broken.
Each day glass thins in the frames,
salt from the bay below rusts the door lock.
Shadow-laughter fades up through the skylight
where full moon once captured diamond-bright,
a ring of iced glitter through the slate roof.
Outside snow fell, uncharacteristic on Atlantic shores.
Whiter-than-white the wash of it seemed limitless,
merged in silence between the gardenia glaze
of moonlight and sky's frozen breath.

Rocks walls built to hold the family in
carve into the wounded blue day,
breaking to fragments the distance between past and present.
Winter's shortening days dust the rooms.
Empty. Of everything but candle butts
burned down in the nights of our company.
Empty. Of the clutter of teenage mayhem –
b-b-q, sundeck chairs, wood-drift from the pebbled beach
collected as a hoard of treasure even stone walls could not protect.
Everything that was light-filled was being rendered obsolete,
while we friends, unknowing, went about our plans,
this loss unimagined, impossible.
I think of you locked out, walking there now,
past the house echoing something almost memory
under the night-blue absence of the moon.

The Busy Sky at Five am

Errislannan

> *...but some of us are looking at the stars*
> — Oscar Wilde

Stars are falling into a lough so still its reeds are
struck to silence, water a mirror's meniscus
slick with mercurial night. Above, the sky is alive.
Orion's belt is swinging, links flickering like fireflies
teasing-up his desire to reach the glittering women
of the Pleiades braiding their shimmering tresses.
Slyne Head lighthouse pulses its mechanical
double-beat across coral-white sands,
stretches out over skies and oceans beyond sight
to calm restless ships. Navigation lights on the wings of a plane
in mimicry of Christmas, switch green and red
in a shale sky as it heads north toward gleaming
arctic crags. It weaves between a scatter of piercing stars,
sparse tonight because that full blaze of a Hunter's moon,
dipping low to the west to set in this breath-held October night,
outshines even light.

Once – Again – Still

SAS, November 2014

If you could place your palm
soft and flat between my breasts
lying here in dawn,
as you did when want was greater
than only flesh,
there would be huge heat.
I'm sure of it.

You raced into my dream again
as if we were young,
couldn't look away from each other
urgent with a kind of wonder,
blue everywhere –
skies, eyes, lake, the future.

That blaze
simply at the presence of you
lingers with me into daylight,
foolish, unexpected,
with no possible path before it.
Yes, it *was* love.
Just love.

Night is passing away.
I soak into this dream
as long as I can, smiling,
brim-full with it, before day
opens its eyes to steal it,
streaming in with its curious light.

Living here alone and content,
except for the ache in my hand,
fingers curling into old age
as yours do, every inch of my skin is
soft with you, flooded with you
as if you were here.

Thirty years. And I miss that
coursing through my veins,
that too-alive flesh. I want to
feel it again – hunger, its purity –
that longing. Then, appeased by touch –
tasting of fate and truth –
before anything was wretched and lost –

feel that drench of dreadful love.

The gods gave it to me once –
                    out of kindness I suppose.

The Light House

at the house of Grace and Michéal, Drimeen

Three swallows follow me swooping down your lane,
their flicker of black-blue gleam diving at the car then flitting
above scarlet fuchsia. At first your house seems empty, or really,
filled with your absence – and his – the children – all three.

Things are missing – the purple shawl I gave you for
colder times, a fluted candle-holder, its glass flowers
budding flame, silver onyx earrings hanging from a small
old-fashioned model on the dresser.

Silence at first is a sinuous creature, arms reaching
in supplication, begging for sound, even dispute.
Then sunlit day surrounds me in the kitchen where
large new windows draw in the sea below, a match with

forget-me-nots sprouting along the gravel path beside red clover.
Sorrel is flowering, foxgloves strung with violet bells.
Red valerian and white daisies are remnants of that year your field blew
wild with flowers that strangely never again exploded into colour.

Light flows in through the front room, glass on three sides,
pushing its face to the salt. The green field out front
running down towards the bog and sea-rocks
is spinning its lime-green twill across late afternoon.

Rooms shuffle around me, settling. Mannin makes a perfect
reflection – you could walk on water – its coral strand
two broad lips, hinting, sea the taut sheen of a barely-blue
evening dress pulled too tight across the hips.

Nights already so short of darkness are edging days
toward summer solstice. Full moon is brimming through
the pentagonal upstairs bedroom window as I ready for bed,
capturing me wide-eyed inside its starry blaze.

Pulsing swan-white, it is sailing horizontal with the sea.
So much light – a sky full of shining, a sea burnished
to a river of foil across Ceann Dólainn bay. The tide is
pushing it out towards the open Atlantic, pulling sleep with it.

Everything is polished silver. Naked skin,
the field before the house is shivering
delighted under its glaze. I keep rising to watch it.
Grazing through the glass, I can't fill myself enough on it.

Honeysuckle I picked from the hedgerow
is sending its scent through the house,
rising up the stairs as the moon becomes that flower,
turning deep yellow, finally blushing rose as dawn uncloaks it.

A sliver of cloud passes like a vein across her
opening as her blue shadows spread, fading her away.
More swallows are gathering out front, acrobats of summer
delighting in their arrival after the exhaustion of flight.

Travelling from here to Spain, France, over Morocco and the Sahara,
they have visited Mecca, eaten insects from Irish cattle, African buffalo.
Swinging back, tugged by invisible threads from the place of their beginning,
after all their wandering, they return home.

Your house is humming with light as I leave,
amber day pouring itself in. More than just things it holds.
Walls contain history, laughter. Everything you have built remains,
waiting for you, airy and open; love stirring in and out of shadow.

Singing up Stone

for Iris and Michael & the sculptor Jayne Woodfield

From scattered remains of a ruin you built this house back into itself
balanced on land's edge beyond Boatharbour. You named it Clochán,
'a pile of stones'. Into the granite of Connemara, you fixed a wide
window at gable's end to watch bluebells shaking their colour into the sea.

Because things are settled here into the land
by the way of the wind and the draw of the sea
you will have known you were returning circle to rocky circle,
bringing sea-life back from stone when you brought the carving.

It sits in your garden inside a ring of rough grey rocks
heavy with a lace of white lichen
beside the fairy mound that shivers without breeze
protected from wild Atlantic gales by a fuchsia hedge.

'Oolite' limestone hatched from the Hellenic word for egg,
spherical grains of concentric layers, even-textured,
compacted over thousands of years with ocean bones
to press themselves into Ancaster Weatherbed.

Smooth burl of shell and sand fragments
from shallow sea-beds where they lay thousands of years before,
buff coloured and blue, grey and creamy amber,
it's a stone to be rolled, shaped, polished and touched.

The sculptor took a sleek form from inside the limestone,
shaving aside its dross like Michelangelo with his Carrara,
carving out the nautilus curled inside,
unleashing sensuality from petrified ages.

In life, 'living fossil', 'sailor', this nautilus is stone-caught, land-laid.
You can run your hand inside its whorl, fingers
sliding down its slick surface, lick-able,
hip-smooth, shoulder-round, belly-curved, palm-cupped.

In this home you have sung up from a forgotten house,
turf is black, rhubarb red, candelabra-primula grows cerise.
Plates are cobalt and white, spirals subtle on fork and spoon.
Everything here is clear, placed carefully, intended.

'Now we have the Three Treasures of our garden,' you say:
daffodils sun-yellow beside a whale spine-bone green with moss;
an indigo plate your son gave you spilling rainwater; and
the nautilus, sailing still. And – I add a fourth, inside Clochán – you.

Ecstasy – A Seaweed Bath…

for Eileen Keane

seaweed shine in our hair
skin smooth as a seal's
scars gleaming and well-worn
your ringlets black as a mermaid's,
travelling Leenane to Letterfrack
trying for words for what colour
is that amethyst mauve of rhododendrons,
gold-bright glitter of gorse beside,
whiter-than-white light on the Bens'
bare quartz bones, and loughs full of trees
in an upside-down sky swimming there.
Sean Keane is singing Dylan's and Adele's
'Make You Feel My Love',
where you could be happy
dreams might come true,
and all this time we're living it –
the colour, the music, the pea-green land
and the unshakeable cello-deep
thrum of friendship.
We babble about words, writing, music,
we sing and sing ourselves from exhaustion to
elation, and think of men we'd like to –
love – and still, after I drop you home,
rising high on it all, I'm feeling –
we could rule the world, friend! We could!

Departure, Connemara

Windows are dark now, black panes.
Only a lingam of candle-flame moves
totally gold, upright against the stone hearth.
Full moon will later gild the lough below the house.
Earlier it was full of clouds,
a porthole of window stuffed blue with sky
then burning, flaming with the sun's red breath.
Walking, I could hear only myself
step on the uneven boreen,
dodging small dips of mud left from the downpour,
bog beside squeezing itself dry again.
Stopping, silence had come in on the land,
evening air loaded with nothing but light
until white bull-calves returned to munching,
tearing the bright green grass out by its roots.
I paused to pick blackberries
fingers blood-red with the crush
though usually they leave their mark fig-purple.
Maybe I'm earlier this year – there was no bitter taste.

And yet I'm tired of all the coming and going.

The Line of Drift

There's a sad whisper in the mist over the sea
as it tumbles stone careless on Drimeen.
Silence carries it across the lough's slick face
washed of tears, moon a fat half all gold.
Cinching its waist, a green ring travels with it
like a promise round a half-true bright thing.

There's a melancholy moan from a calf in the field.
Slyne Head flashes twice,
the beat of two pulses close in a dance.
Night is dark and thick without stars
and the few front windows still alight
across bog hills glow yellow,
souls still up and walking their hallways, sleepless.

Perhaps they too had too much good company,
were caught in laughter mid-way to something
barely sensed, had their own barbed-wire walls
so firmly pinioned to contentment,
they also were jolted into wakefulness
by the chances life might give.

My unexpected guest, you come knocking again,
with your red shoes and wild blue eyes.
Unplanned, we wonder why the road draws us together,
why tiredness does not weary the sound of our voices.
We talk the night old, laughing at ourselves,
but never at the deep things,
moments of connection that really count,
that make sinews and bone sing
no matter how short the time and fleeting.

The land is dark now.
Below, the loughs are quiet and calm
they need no stormy tides of desire,
no rusted hopes to stir their reedy silence.
Wearied at last, just before dawn sheds her shadows,
we part with the wind rising, tearing at your jacket.

I remember the feel of it as we hugged,
my arm sliding beneath it along your ribs.
Loose and keen it flew out under the dark sky
though heavy it was, an assured kind of weight,
baubley to the fingertips, grey and black,
slub and sleek places, over muscle, fur and flesh.

Funny the things we remember:
'just old' you said, but I found myself in envy of it,
those years of closeness,
the times it hung into its separate life
knowing days would come
when it wound you round
in a holding full of comfort.

The small indigo glass heart I gave you
was in its pocket.
And that's all there was.

Now, the moon moves on over
and will halve again and grow small
the way boats grow small carrying passengers away,
who themselves, caught into their skins,
are changed on parting,
taking something of us with them,
the distance between shore and ship ever-increasing
until the speck of hull is vacant horizon.

You will be driving through the dark country, home
everything there settled and set to place.
Yet I am always in this state of departing,
of leaving behind.
That's what came to me down the line –
a small rip in the fabric of the heart
ever remembered on parting –
and the distance between two shores.

ABOUT THE AUTHOR

ROBYN ROWLAND is an Irish-Australian dual-citizen, annually visiting for thirty-three years, now living half-time in Connemara. She has written twelve books, nine of poetry. Her most recent is the bi-lingual book *This Intimate War: Gallipoli/Çanakkale 1915 — İçli Dışlı Bir Savaş: Gelibolu/ Çanakkale 1915*, with Turkish translations by Mehmet Ali Çelikel, published in Australia and Turkey, 2015. *Seasons of doubt & burning. New & Selected Poems* (Five Islands Press, Melbourne, 2010) represented forty years of work.

Her other books are: *Silence & its Tongues* (Five Islands Press, Melbourne, 2006); *Shadows at the Gate* (Five Islands Press, Wollongong, 2004); *Fiery Waters* (Five Islands Press, Wollongong, 2001); *Perverse Serenity* (Heinemann, Melbourne,1990); and *Filigree in Blood* (Longman Cheshire Modern Poets, Melbourne, 1982).

Robyn's poetry appears in national and international journals and in over thirty-six anthologies, including six *Best Australian Poems*: *2014, 2013, 2010, 2009, 2005* and *2004* (Black Inc.), with editors Les Murray, Robert Adamson, Lisa Gorton and Geoff Page; and *Being Human*, ed. Neil Astley, (Bloodaxe Books, UK, 2011).

Her work has been awarded a number of prizes and she has published and read in Australia, Ireland, Japan, Bosnia, Serbia, Austria, Turkey, Canada, India, New Zealand, Portugal, the UK, the USA, Greece and Italy. Her poetry has been featured on Australian and Irish national radio programs. Robyn has two CDs, *Off the Tongue* and *Silver Leaving — Poems & Harp* with Lynn Saoirse.

Dr Robyn Rowland AO is an Honorary Fellow, School of Culture and Communication, University of Melbourne, Australia; was a member of the National Advisory Council for Australia Poetry Ltd 2010-2013; curated and presented the *Poetry & Conversation* Series for the Geelong Library Corporation, 2010-2013; and was inaugural Deputy Chair of the Board of the Australian Poetry Centre 2007-2009. Previously Professor of Social Inquiry and Women's Studies at Deakin University, she retired in 1996 and was created an Officer in the Order of Australia for her contribution to higher education and women's health.